OTHERS COME TO VIEW THE MONORAIL FROM THE AIR, IN MACHINES WITH A SLIGHTLY LESS PERFECT RECORD...
MAYDAY! TOTAL FAILURE ON ALL ENGINES. NOTHING ELSE FOR IT...

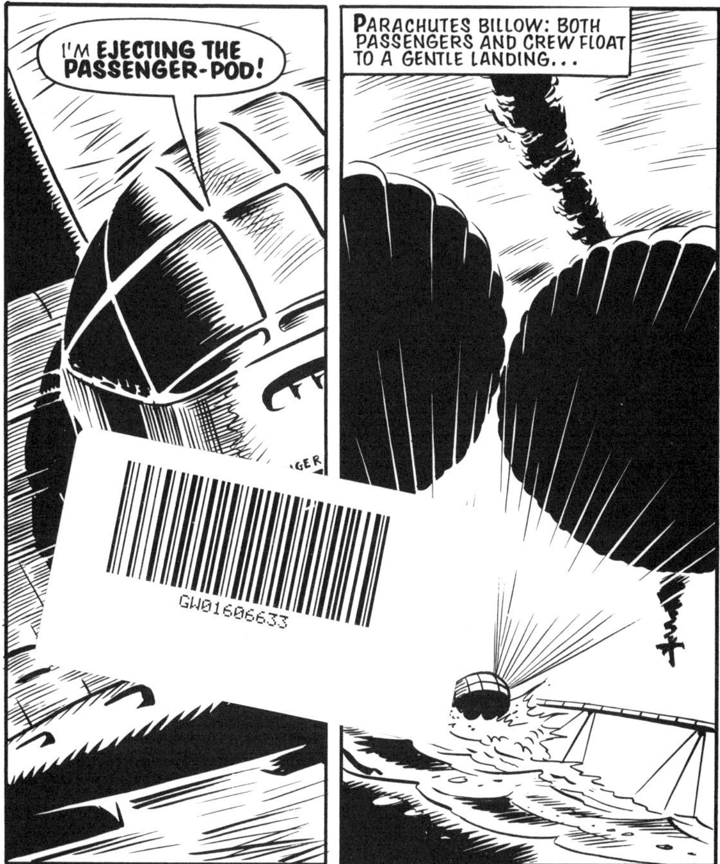
I'M EJECTING THE PASSENGER-POD!
PARACHUTES BILLOW: BOTH PASSENGERS AND CREW FLOAT TO A GENTLE LANDING...

THE PLANE ITSELF DOES NOT!
SHKAK

UNCLE WARREN! THE TUBE'S...

BROKEN!

WITHIN MINUTES, SIGNALS HAVE BEEN FLASHED TO INTERNATIONAL RESCUE'S PACIFIC COMMAND CENTRE, ARCOLOGY...
IT SOUNDS BAD, GRAN...
IT IS, DYLAN BUT AT LEAST THE PLANE-PASSENGERS ARE ALREADY BEING PICKED UP!
AND ONLY ONE MONORAIL CAR'S GONE DOWN IN THE SEA...
BUT THAT CAR JUST HAPPENED TO BE CARRYING...
"COMMANDER SIMPSON AND SKIPPER..."
NOBODY SERIOUSLY HURT AND THE CAR'S STAYED WATER-TIGHT SO FAR...
BUT WE'RE WEDGED INTO THIS CREVICE...
WE'LL BE OKAY, SKIPPER...WE'LL KEEP THE ELECTRIC LIGHTS ON SO WE CAN BE SEEN...
AND THE T-BIRDS'LL PULL US OUT OF THIS, DON'T YOU WORRY I EXPECT THEY'LL BRING...

TB-4, TB-13 AND TB-14... ALL SAFELY STOWED ABOARD!
RIGHT... NEXT STOP, THE MOZAMBIQUE CHANNEL...

WEATHER'S GOOD... NO PROBLEM GETTING THERE...
THE PROBLEMS START AFTER WE ARRIVE... AND THE FIRST ONE'S FINDING THE CAR...
NOW, WITH THE SPEED IT WAS TRAVELLING, AND THE AGULHAS CURRENT RUNNING SOUTH...
I'D SAY WE START LOOKING ABOUT HERE!

AND SOON, OFF THE COAST OF MADAGASCAR...
THUNDERBIRD-4 UNDERWAY! SUBMERGING TO 800 FATHOMS...

AND, FOLLOWING A COMPUTER-CONTROLLED COURSE FOR HALF AN HOUR...
LOOKS LIKE YOU WERE RIGHT, KALLAN...

THERE IT IS, RIGHT UP AHEAD WE'VE FOUND IT!
ONLY TROUBLE IS...
TB-4

SOMETHING ELSE HAS FOUND IT, TOO!
A GIANT SQUID!

THAT THING'S PUTTING SO MUCH PRESSURE ON THE SEALS THEY'RE STARTING TO LEAK!
IT'S NOT SERIOUS YET, BUT IF WE DON'T GET OUT OF THIS SOON...

MAYBE WE CAN SCARE OFF THAT MONSTER IF WE GET IN CLOSE...
IT DOESN'T LOOK SCARED, KALLAN...

NO IT DOESN'T, DOES IT?
OKAY, GUYS HANG ON WHILE I ROLL HER OVER!

AND WE'LL SEE HOW IT LIKES IT WHEN I TURN ON THE ULTRACANDESCENT LIGHTING TROUGHS IN ITS FACE!
THAT DID IT, KALLAN!
RIGHT...AND NOW WE'VE GOT TO MOVE FAST...
"THE CAR'S SLOWLY FILLING WITH WATER..."
EVERYONE GET UP HERE AT THE TOP END!
"AND IT'S JAMMED INTO THOSE ROCKS WITH THE EMERGENCY EXIT AT THE BOTTOM END..."
OKAY, THIS IS WHAT WE DO! DYLAN...

TAKE TB-13 A MILE NORTH AND SPREAD A MILD ANAESTHETIC, SO THE CURRENT CARRIES IT OVER THE WHOLE AREA...
I DON'T WANT TO HAVE TO TANGLE WITH THAT SQUID AGAIN!
THUNDERBIRD-13: MINI-SUB...
AND GRAN, YOU'LL LAUNCH TB-14...
THUNDERBIRD-14: DEEP SEA BATHYSCOPE...
OKAY, THAT'S GOT THE GRAPPLES CLAMPED IN PLACE...
BUT...
NO GOOD, KALLAN! I CAN'T MOVE IT IT'S STUCK TIGHT!
THE ROCK MUST'VE COLLAPSED ONTO IT...
STAY IN POSITION, GRAN...

I'LL SEE IF I CAN SHIFT IT WITH THE **HYDRAULIC RAM!**
GOT TO ANGLE THIS JUST RIGHT...

AND MAKE SURE IT FALLS **AWAY** FROM THE RAIL-CAR!
OKAY, GRAN!

"TAKE IT AWAY!"
GOT IT!

IT'S **FREE**, KALLAN!
WHICH JUST LEAVES ME TO COME ALONGSIDE THE EXIT-DOOR AND PICK UP THE SURVIVORS!
TB-4

AND SOON...
AP-1
GREAT! WE'VE GOT THEM ALL SAFELY INTO THE DECOMPRESSION CHAMBER!
YOU KNOW, MAYBE IT'S A GOOD JOB THEY HAVE TO STAY IN THERE FOR A FEW HOURS...

I DON'T THINK COMMANDER SIMPSON'S GOING TO BE TOO HAPPY...
NOT WHEN THIS HAPPENS ON HIS **DAY OFF!**

Welcome to Wizard World

"Time to put through a routine alert, I think," said Watch-officer Mkale, as he approached the end of his shift on Thunderbird Six. The rest of the team in Operations Control Centre glanced at him briefly and nodded as he started to feed the information into his computer terminal. It would only take a matter of seconds for that warning to flash down from the orbitting space-station to International Rescue's main base in the Pacific.

"A big storm building up in the North Pacific, Commander," announced Gran Hansen as the alert came through. "Weather-control are bombarding it with deionization beams, but there's only so much they can do . . ."

"Right . . . we'll keep an eye on that one," Simpson told him. As usual, they were going through the morning's reports, looking for sources of potential trouble. "What else have we got?"

"Not a lot," Gran told him. "A small bushfire in South Australia. A minor earth-tremor in central China. A ship with its cargo shifting in the Caribbean. Local emergency services seem to have them all pretty much under control . . ."

"Okay, tell TB-6 to keep monitoring all of them in case they need assistance," said Simpson, then allowed himself a slight smile. "Quiet morning, hey, Gran?"

"So far . . ." Gran agreed cautiously. "At least it gives me time to go and get a cup of coffee . . ."

But by the time he'd finished his drink, Officer Mkale had sent a new, and slightly more worrying report.

"Seems that storm has reached the island of Kyushu in southern Japan," Simpson told him. "Weather-control's taken some of the sting out of it, but they couldn't manage to disperse it completely . . ."

"Shouldn't be too much of a problem though, should it?" remarked Gran. "After all, people survived storms before there was weather-control . . ."

"True," admitted Simpson. "But if it's too big for weather-control to deal with . . . well, maybe I'm worrying too much, but I think we'll get everybody taking an early lunch, just in case . . ."

The panic started just before the second course was served.

"Japan?" queried Dylan worriedly as the team dashed into Commander Simpson's office for briefing. "What's happened?"

"We're not sure how bad it is yet," Simpson told him. "It's that giant amusement park in Kyushu, Wizard-World. It seems the main computer that runs the place has been struck by lightning. And . . . well, there's only one way to describe it. The computer's run amok!"

"Well, let's get moving then!" said Dylan urgently. Simpson raised a hand and tried to calm him down.

"We can't make any move until we've got more details," he told him. "We don't know exactly what the situation is yet . . ."

"But listen, I was born in Japan!" protested Dylan. "There might be friends of mine involved!"

"We might *all* have friends involved," put in Gran. "But you know the score, Dylan . . . we can't allow personal feelings to come into this. Every rescue has to be treated exactly the same . . ."

"Yeah, you're right," agreed Dylan. "Still . . ."

"Still, I can't see that we'll be needing TB-1 on a mission like this," said Simpson quietly. "So you may as well take Thunderbird Ten and get out there fast, Dylan. It usually helps to have a man on the spot so we know exactly what's going on . . ."

"Great!" said Dylan, dashing away immediately, and then pausing briefly at the door. "And thank you, Commander . . ."

A mere fifteen minutes later, Dylan brought the mini-rocketship in to make a perfect vertical landing about a quarter of a mile from the perimeter of Wizard-World. By then the heart of the storm had moved on, a mass of lightning-slashed thunderheads which rumbled and growled in the distance, though it was still raining heavily. But getting wet was the last thing Dylan was worried about as he leaped to the ground and went looking for someone to give him a situation report.

"It's hard to make an estimate," said Captain Kojima of the local police force. "Our guess is that there were about four thousand people in the park before the storm struck, but the central computer's got the only record of how many admissions there were. And *that's* not going to give us any help. We've got most of those people out . . . at least three thousand anyway . . . and more are coming out all the time."

"But do you know what's happening inside?" asked Dylan, opening a channel on his portable radio so the information would go back direct to Arcology.

"That's the problem," Kojima told him. "We tried to fly a surveillance 'copter over the place a few minutes ago, but the computer's refashioned the laser light-displays into weapons. Our 'copter was shot down before it could send back any pictures . . ."

Dylan groaned quietly as they walked toward the park. "Has anyone been in on the ground?"

"It's closed off all the gates in the perimeter fence . . . except one which we've managed to force open with a barricade of police trucks. But it keeps trying to push our trucks out of the way with cars from the 'Hi-Speed Thrill-o-rama' exhibit. But we're holding our own at the moment. That's where most of the survivors are coming out . . ."

"Okay, I'll need all the maps, diagrams, blueprints and so on that you can get me," Dylan told him. "Any deaths or injuries?"

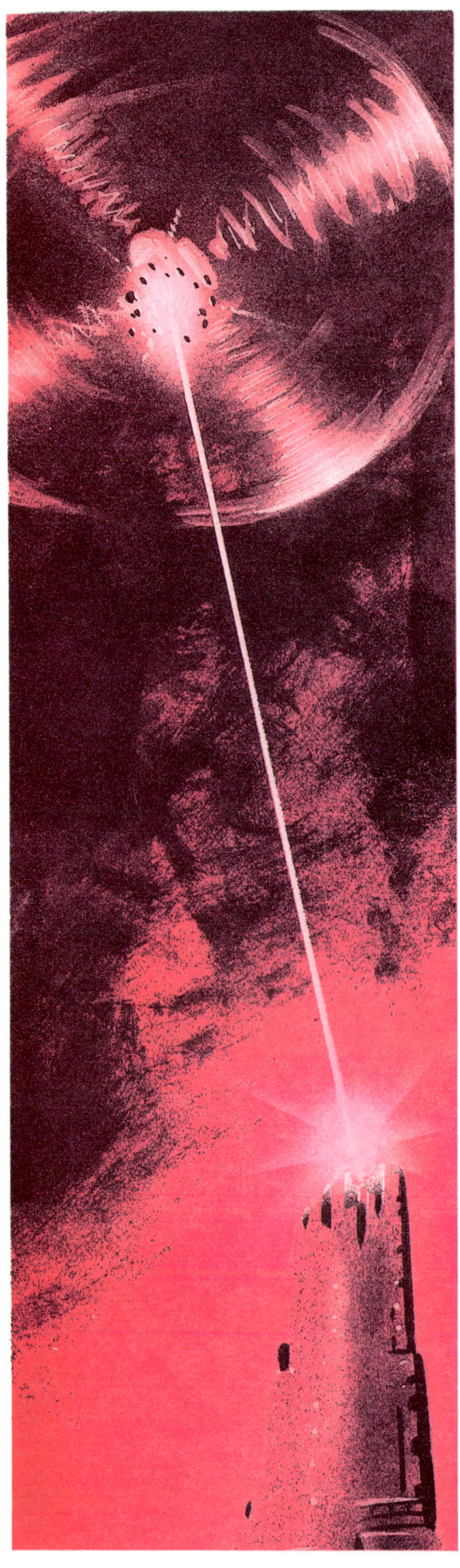

"We don't know of any deaths, but we've got fifty-seven people with various injuries, mostly minor. One or two with bad cuts . . . and there's a rumour that the robot Samurai from the history display have got loose . . . which is another reason why I'm not sending my men in there . . .!"

By then they had arrived at the large police-truck which was serving as a temporary headquarters, parked not far from the perimeter fence, and Kojima immediately started getting the maps. Dylan took a quick look at the general ground-plan, and then put through a call to Commander Simpson.

"The trouble is," he began, "there are so many different types of problem we could run up against that it's hard to guess what equipment we'll need. I'd say that, apart from TB-2 and TB-3, we could want Thunderbirds 5, 11, 12, 13, 15 and 16 . . ."

"That's more or less what we guessed," came Simpson's voice over the radio. "And everything's been loaded aboard TB-2 and is already on its way . . . except for TB-13. We didn't think you'd be needing a mini-sub on dry land . . ."

"I'm *hoping* we don't," Dylan told him. "But there's an artificial lake here called 'Underwater World'. Seems that visitors ride along the bottom in small railcars . . . and if anyone's stuck down there . . ."

"Right," agreed Simpson. "Fastest way we can get it to you is to load it onto Thunderbird 8 and fly it out by remote control. But it'll take at least an hour to reach you . . ."

"And TB-2?"

"Twenty minutes . . . it left shortly after you did . . ."

"So now what do we do . . . wait?" asked Kojima worriedly.

"Yes and no," Dylan told him. "We wait for the equipment, but in the meantime, let's get all the men you can spare onto questioning people who've escaped. I want to hear from anyone who thinks he knows where people might be trapped in there . . ."

By the time the rest of the Thunderbirds team arrived, Dylan had a somewhat better idea of what was going on.

"Our first problem is getting in," he

said, pointing to the map as the others gathered round in Kojima's truck. "We can't go in by air or we'll be shot down, so it looks like we're going to have to force our way in through the one gate that's left open. Now, there might be a bunch of robots running around with samurai swords, so we'll all carry sidearms, right? And watch out for any cars or other movable machinery . . . the computer's quite likely to be using them as weapons . . ."

"After that," said Gran, "I guess our main task is going to be knocking out that blasted computer . . ."

"Right," agreed Dylan. "But when they built this place they decided to put the computer on an island in the centre of the park and surround it with a moat and fence to make sure no one could interfere with it. It's got low-frequency sound disruptors to warn off anyone who tries to cross the moat, and wide-beam stun-blasters to knock out people who don't listen. And of course, now it's got lasers too . . ."

"So it's like breaking into a fortress," said Little John thoughtfully. "Anyone trapped anywhere?"

"All we know for sure is that three people are dangling on wires from the practice parachute-jump tower," Dylan told him. "And it looks like there's a car stuck inside the 'Ride through a Human Body' exhibit."

"The *what?*" asked Jesse.

"The giant figure lying along the hillside here," explained Dylan, pointing to the map. "It's like a huge biology lesson. The customers travel through the inside of the body in cars, starting from the mouth. It seems there's a car stuck, probably somewhere in the small intestine. I guess we're going to have to go in through the side of the stomach, and then just sort of feel around until we find something . . ."

"I'm glad you're not my doctor, Dylan!" smiled Kallan.

"ENJOY YOURSELVES!" boomed a colossal voice over Wizard-World's public address system. "YOU *WILL* ENJOY YOURSELVES . . . OR YOU WILL BE *PUNISHED!* NO ONE ELSE LEAVES HERE UNTIL THEY *HAVE* ENJOYED THEMSELVES! THERE IS NO CHOICE!"

"You *sure* we've got to go in there, fellas?" asked Jesse.

Gran nodded. "Like it says . . . there's no choice . . ."

A couple of minutes later they were ready to begin. Gran remained behind in TB-3 to co-ordinate things and run any of the remote-control vehicles they might need to use; and also to consult the mobile computer if the situation should arise. Little John and Kallan took their seats in TB-5 and Dylan in TB-11. Jesse's first task would be to bulldoze a way in for them with TB-12.

Extending Thunderbird-12's huge power-shovel and broadcasting a warning to any police or civilians that might be in the way on the loud-hailer, Jesse nosed the huge flat-bed through the gateway and started to slowly shove aside the barricade of trucks. He came under attack almost straight away.

"YOU HAVE NOT PAID YOUR ADMISSION FEE!" roared the voice of the central computer, as one of the Hi-Speed cars hurtled toward the flat-bed and smashed itself against the shovel-blade. Jesse pushed

that aside too, wondering how many more cars it might have to throw away.

It seemed that the answer was only one more, for the last of the kamikaze cars plastered itself all over the shovel just as Jesse removed the last of the obstructions. For the moment at least, an open roadway lay before them, leading toward the centre of the park.

Dylan brought Thunderbird-11 alongside, and Jesse gave him a brief wave of acknowledgement as they started toward the computer island. Kallan and Little John, meanwhile, turned away up a side-path and started toward the Human Body. Behind them, more tourists straggled toward freedom.

Jesse and Dylan had not gone much farther before they ran into more problems, though. At one side of the park a new exhibit was due to be built, showing miniature versions of the seven ancient Wonders of the World, and the ground was just being cleared. Now the computer decided to bring one of the huge robot bulldozers into the action.

"Hey, Dylan!" yelled Jesse into the radio as he saw the machine approach, the weight of the thing causing its caterpillar treads to break up the surface of the road as it lumbered forward. It was almost as big as Thunderbird-12 itself. "If I get into a head-on confrontation with that thing, I'm not sure who's going to come out best!"

"I see it, Jesse," Dylan told him, flicking on TB-11's computer-controlled sensors and starting to look for a weak-spot in the approaching machine. Then, moving slightly off to one side, Dylan lined up his lasers on the bulldozer's caterpillar treads and opened fire.

The treads parted with whip-crack snap and the lumbering machine slewed round, going off the road and piling into a nearby pavilion, destroying the building utterly before it finally ground to a halt.

"Nice shooting, partner!" Jesse told him as they manoeuvred round the rubble and continued on their way.

As Kallan and Little John weren't moving directly toward the centre of the park, the computer apparently decided that they posed no direct threat to it, and they

managed to reach the Human Body exhibit without too much trouble. It was only when they started forcing their way in through the plastic skin that the computer responded.

"THIS IS AN ACT OF VANDALISM!" it roared, as TB-5 disappeared within. "YOU ARE INTRUDING UPON A RESTRICTED AREA!"

"I never realised a human body looked like *this!*" exclaimed Little John as he stared at the mass of electrical gear and machinery that lay before them.

"We're behind the scenes, remember?" said Kallan. "Only those parts that the public see actually look like the real thing. All this stuff is what makes it work . . ."

A small flame sprang up somewhere to their right, then spread rapidly along the cable-insulation like a fiery spider's web.

"It's set the place on fire!" yelled Little John, hitting the accelerator and driving their vehicle forward through the blazing machinery. A few moments later they broke through another plastic wall and found themselves on the tracks of the car-ride itself.

"Which way now?" asked Little John, as the flames started to grow more fierce. The heat wouldn't worry them within their efficiently insulated shell of Mandellium, but the car they were hoping to find would be much more vulnerable.

"That way!" pointed Kallan. "This is the large intestine . . . we have to go through this to reach the small one . . ."

Little John drove Thunderbird-5 through the eerily glistening plastic tunnel as fast as he dared, then rather faster as the walls themselves started first to smoulder and then to burst into flame. The fire kept following them as they moved out of the large intestine and into the small.

A couple of minutes later, with the tunnel now full of acrid black smoke, they found the car they were looking for. It was little more than a clear plastic bubble that ran along the rails, and the three American tourists inside were starting to look distinctly panicstricken as the flames roared around them.

"We can't pull them out of there in this inferno!" said Kallan worriedly.

"Only one thing to do," Little John told her. "We'll have to run up behind it and then push it along until we reach the exit . . ."

"Right," agreed Kallan. "And I'll use the forward extinguishers to keep the car cool until we can set them free. But let's keep it moving fast . . ."

Dylan and Jesse had been moving swiftly too, and by now they had reached the moat that surrounded the central island.

"YOU ARE A THREAT TO THE SECURITY OF THIS PARK!" the computer warned them. "YOU WILL BE DESTROYED!"

"Let's do it now, Jesse!" Dylan said, reversing away from the moat and scanning the computerbuilding for it's most vulnerable point. "It looks like it's trying to gear those display lasers downwards so it can use them as ground-level weapons against us . . ."

"You just get yourself a good run-up!" Jesse told him, as he operated the extending platform, moving it back and tilting it down behind TB-12. As soon as it was in position,

Dylan hit the accelerator and sent TB-11 roaring forward.

Using TB-12's platform as a ramp, Dylan sent his car hurtling through the air at maximum speed, a leap which carried him clear across the moat and onto the island beyond. His forward lasers where blazing even before the front wheels hit the ground.

The computer's wide-beam stun-blasters were useless against TB-11's armour, though the sonic disruptors did cause Dylan a moment's discomfort before he was past them. Bracing himself in the driving seat, Dylan kept the car going at full speed.

"STOP!" screamed the computer, an almost human note of desperation in its voice. Dylan wasn't listening.

The lasers had already weakened the wall before the car's armoured nose hit the concrete with boneshaking impact. The jolt was so savage that Dylan almost lost consciousness, but by the time he realised what was happening the car was through the wall and he was inside the building. The massive computer lay before him, relays clicking and lights flashing dementedly.

Dylan was in no mood for subtlety; he knew he had to get this over with before the computer had time to come up with a new means of defence. Keeping his foot hard down on the accelerator, he drove the car forward until it ground into the sparking mass of electronics, then opened the forward ports and lobbed out grenades in all directions, hunching in his seat as he waited for the explosions.

An electronic whine that sounded almost like a scream echoed over the blasts, and then the room was plunged into darkness save for a few small flames. As the place started to fill with smoke, Dylan reversed Thunderbird-11 back out of the hole by which he'd entered and looked around at the park. Everything was now completely still.

"It's all over then?" asked Jesse when Dylan rejoined the others.

"All over with the computer," Dylan agreed, looking up as the sun started to come out. "But *our* job's just beginning! Now that the system's been shut down, we're going to have to check out every ride and display in the place to make sure that no one's still trapped . . ."

"And get down those three people dangling on wires," Kallan reminded him.

"Right," nodded Dylan, then smiled. "Still, look on the bright side . . . at least we never ran into those robot samurai!"

January 20, 2086

TO: THE WORLD FEDERATION

FROM: THE UNITED LEAGUE OF NATIONS

RE: INTERNATIONAL RESCUE ORGANIZATION

Mankind is ever expanding the frontiers of technical superiority to areas unknown and uncharted. This never ending quest continually pushes research and development into the increasingly challenging fields of space exploration, energy development, and the biological and environmental sciences. Each area promises marvellous discoveries, but each also brings potential danger.

In direct response to the dangers of our advanced technology, we have developed an organization that is ready to mobilize dramatic survival resources at a moment's notice, to spearhead dangerous missions, and to answer last chance distress calls that can arrive any time from any disaster scene on or off this planet.

That organization is INTERNATIONAL RESCUE. The specialized rescue squad is the THUNDERBIRDS. A team that combines five of the finest cadets in the world, chosen for their physical and intellectual abilities, dedicated to the service of Mankind wherever he may be in distress with a dazzling array of vehicles and equipment designed to specifications as yet unconceived in the space-age technology of the 21st century.

Conceptions in rescue that challenge the impossible, defying perilous odds again and again with complete disregard for the risks. THUNDERBIRDS 2086.

ARCOLOGY

Earth Base Command Centre located on a remote island in the Pacific.

TOTAL PRESENT:	55,505
UNRESTRICTED VISITORS IN MALL:	5,665
VISITORS WITH SPECIAL PASSES:	1,711
NON-RESIDENT WORKERS:	321
UNAUTHORIZED VISITORS:	0
DETAINED PRISONERS:	0
DESIGN GOAL:	100,000
NOW RESIDENT:	60,453
RESIDENT IN OUTBUILDINGS:	765

The ARCOLOGY is a vast city complex housed on about four square miles of buildings and grounds. The main building is a thousand feet high, rising from a square mile base, one-half mile on a side.

Dr. Warren Simpson

AGE: 55
RANK: COMMANDER
PLACE OF BIRTH: WASHINGTON, D.C.

STATS: The chief engineer and designer of the INTERNATIONAL RESCUE ORGANIZATION and former NASA astronaut. Degrees in: Aerospace Engineering, Industrial Engineering and Systems Engineering. Expertise in: Astrophysics and Geophysics. His last post was Commander of the research spacecraft UNSS CLARKE. He has hand chosen the rest of the INTERNATIONAL RESCUE ORGANIZATION team.

Primary responsibility: Commander-in-chief of the INTERNATIONAL RESCUE ORGANIZATION. Reports directly to THE WORLD FEDERATION SUPREME COUNCIL.

Dylan Beyda

AGE: 28
RANK: CAPTAIN
PLACE OF BIRTH: TOKYO

STATS: Son of the famous space explorer, Harrison Beyda. Dylan's natural leadership abilities make him the spokesperson for the group. Graduate of Yale and Oxford Universities. Degrees in: Astronomy and Quantum Mechanics. Expertise in: Crystallography and Navigation. Proficient in karate and tai chi.

Primary responsibility: Pilot, TB-1.

Gran Hanson

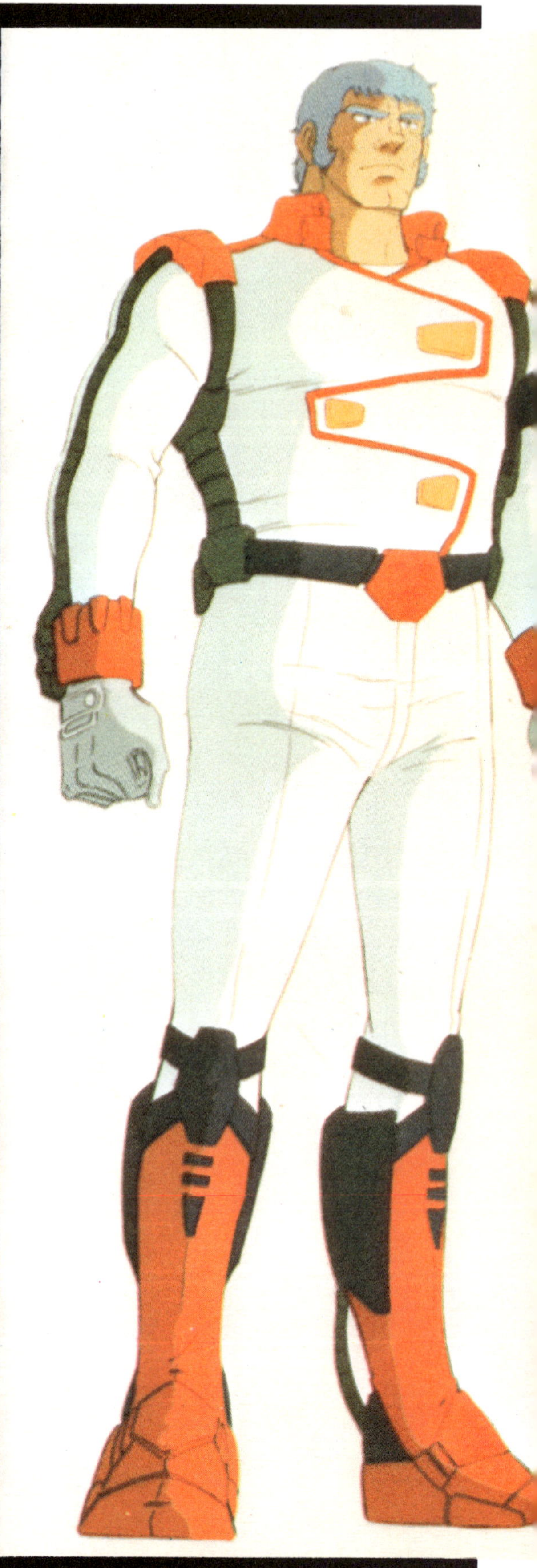

AGE: 45
RANK: CAPTAIN; SENIOR OFFICER
PLACE OF BIRTH: NEW BERLIN

STATS: Trained at Lunar Academy; asteroid miner for RAMA SPACE SEED project. Degrees in: Communications, Fluid Mechanics and Meteorology. Expertise in: Lasers, ion-engines, asteroid geology and weaponry.

Primary responsibility: Pilot, TB-3.

Jesse Rigel

AGE: 29
RANK: CAPTAIN
PLACE OF BIRTH: LUNAR COLONY 9

STATS: Born on the moon but raised in Texas, he fancies himself a space cowboy. Trained at NASA Headquarters, Houston. Degrees in: Aerospace Engineering, Geophysics and Metallurgy. Expertise in Cytology. Ace pilot.

Primary responsibility: Copilot, TB-2.

Kallan James

AGE: 26
RANK: CAPTAIN
PLACE OF BIRTH: SAN DIEGO, CA.

STATS: Graduate of UCLA. Degrees in: Biochemistry and Oceanography. Expertise in: Biophysics, Ecology and Zoology. Olympic swimming Gold Medal Winner (400-metre backstroke), 2076.

Primary responsibility: Pilot, TB-4.

Johnathan Jordan, Jr.

AGE: 30
RANK: CAPTAIN
PLACE OF BIRTH: NEW YORK CITY

STATS: Graduate of NYU. Degrees in: Industrial Engineering and Particle Physics. Expertise in: Archeology and Architecture. Olympic gymnast, Gold Medal Winner 2076.

Primary responsibility: Copilot, TB-2.

Paul 'Skipper' Simpson

AGE: 7

Commander Simpson's nephew. Honorary member of the INTERNATIONAL RESCUE ORGANIZATION team. Hopes to be a space explorer.

Primary responsibility: Attends third grade at the Arcology Elementary School.

A World to Ransom

As the space-tug moved slowly away from Orbital Station 23 and started to accelerate, the pilot looked back with a thin metallic smile of subdued triumph. Why he should feel any emotion about his success he had no idea . . . it had all been far too easy . . . but nonetheless he did. Still, emotions were for later; right now all that mattered was that the first part of the plan had been completed.

Orbital Station 23 receded slowly into the distance as the tug picked up speed; a gleaming metal and glassite ball whirling perpetually around the Earth, its robot crew performing their endless tasks with neither error nor complaint. And totally ignorant of the fact that someone had manually over-ridden their control circuits for the last half an hour, before returning them to their normal duties. But half an hour had been enough. Now it merely remained to move on to the second phase of the plan, and within twenty-four hours, he would be ready to deliver his ultimatum.

That ultimatum was delivered at precisely ten o'clock the following morning. By 10:02, the details had been relayed to Commander Warren Simpson of the International Rescue Organisation, at their Pacific island base, Arcology. By 10:05, the entire Thunderbirds team was assembled for briefing, and already time was starting to slip away too fast.

"As you all know," Simpson began grimly. "Both disease and warfare have been virtually wiped out on this planet. But as you also know, diseases which have been 'officially' wiped out, like smallpox and bubonic plague, have a surprising tendency to reappear just when we're least expecting it. So naturally we keep a small quantity of the original virus for each disease for research, and to prepare vaccines from if needed. Those stocks of virus were kept out in space aboard Orbital Station 23 where they couldn't do any harm . . ."

"*Were* kept there?" asked Dylan.

"Yes, *were* kept there," nodded Simpson. "Along with a quantity of poisonous material left over from the last century when various nations were stockpiling toxic weapons for defence purposes. Even poisons have their uses on occasion, so they were stockpiled there too.

But now it seems that someone has managed to penetrate the Station's security system and make off with large quantities of poison and virus . . ."

Simpson paused for a moment, watching the horrified reactions of his crew before continuing. "Now the World Federation has received an ultimatum: it seems that whoever's responsible for the theft has placed two devices, somewhere on Earth. One, apparently in the sea, contains the toxic material; the other, on land, contains the diseases. And if the Federation doesn't hand over government of the entire planet to this anonymous malefactor within twelve hours, those devices will release their contents. I need hardly tell you what the consequences will be; death for every living thing in the world . . ."

"It must be a bluff!" drawled Jesse. "It's gotta be . . . what would the guy gain by destroying the world?"

"It *might* be a bluff," agreed Simpson. "But we've got to assume he means it. He's certainly got the potential to do it. Now, the World Federation will be delaying its answer until the last moment, so that leaves us eleven hours and fifty minutes to find those devices and make them safe. We've been given Priority Override: any resources we need are available, any information is accessible . . ."

With that they moved into the main communications room, and the team split up to take their positions at various consoles, ready to tap in to the world's computer network.

"Okay, I've got a few suggestions," began Dylan. "First, I guess we've got to assume that our enemy isn't on Earth at the moment. But just in case he is, let's ban all ships leaving for the next twelve hours. If he can't get away himself, he might not pull that switch . . ."

"Consider it done," said Simpson, reaching for a direct visiphone connection to the World Federation.

"Next thing we need to know is when the stuff was taken from Orbital Station 23," Dylan continued, turning to Little John, who had access to that information. "The place is run entirely by robots, and there's a stun-screen on the main airlock to prevent any humans entering. So the robbery must have been carried out by a robot, right?"

"I guess so, Dylan," agreed Little John as the information began to come through on his screen. "They have regular stock checks every week; the last was three days ago, and nothing was missing then. They're carrying out another one right now. Only one ship's docked at the Station since then, and that was a regular service-tug, yesterday noon."

"Then that must have been it," Dylan concluded.

"If it was," Little John said, "whoever's responsible must be some sort of robotics genius. All the robots not involved in the stock-check are having their service-recorders examined; and so far they show absolutely nothing unusual for yesterday . . ."

"I've got records of fourteen ships landing on Earth since yesterday noon," put in Kallan. "All of them with passenger-lists and cargo manifests apparently in order. Federal agents are starting an investigation of each ship, but it'll take . . . well, longer than we've got . . ."

"Oh, good grief . . ." muttered Little John softly as the result of the stock-check flashed up on his screen. "I sure hope this guy's bluffing, because he can do everything he says he can. He's got just about every foul disease and poison you can think of in concentrated form . . . enough to destroy the planet twenty times over . . . and the whole lot weighs less than three kilos . . ."

"Three kilos?" Simpson said thoughtfully. "Forget the big ships, Kallan. Give us a read-out on any debris, old satellites, space-junk, meteors, or whatever may have fallen in the last twenty-four hours. If the stuff weighs that little, he could be sending it down in small automatic missiles . . ."

"Four," replied Kallan after a moment. "South Atlantic, 3:15PM yesterday. North Pacific, 11:20PM. Canada, 11:33PM. Saudi Arabia, 04:00AM this morning. We can only guess the location of each fall to within about twenty miles . . ."

"The middle two," suggested Dylan. "The Pacific and Canada . . . close together both in distance and time."

"That's my guess too," said Simpson. "Jesse and Little John, head north in

TB-2 . . . you can put Kallan and TB-4 down at that Pacific location, then head on to Canada with Gran and TB-3. Assist Gran until you hear from Kallan, and take along all the extra equipment you're likely to need. And remember, the stuff we're looking for is *dangerous!*''

"On our way," said Jesse as he and the others got to their feet and raced into action.

"And what about me?" asked Dylan.

"You and I'll stay here and see if we can work out where to find this madman," Simpson told him. "In case the others can't find his poisons . . ."

At 11:54AM, TB-4 was released into the wide Pacific, and Kallan immediately took the submarine down toward the bottom. Within minutes she had arrived at the position where the object was estimated to have landed, but a factor of twenty miles in the calculations left her an awful lot of sea-bed to search; and that was without taking into account how the ocean-currents might have diverted the object as it sank.

Kallan released the mini-sub, TB-13, on automatic pilot, and the two craft began a

linked search pattern. Even so, Kallan knew as she watched the detector-screens, it was going to be a difficult task. And one she had to complete within the next four or five hours if it was to be any use.

At 12:40PM, TB-2 and TB-3 arrived at their destination in Canada, and found that the search area was right in the middle of a thick pine forest. They too split up and began to search, with Gran using TB-3's jets to skim low over the trees. But their task was to prove just as difficult as Kallan's: she had a vast expanse of deep blue ocean to search . . . the others had a sea of thickly clustered pines . . .

Back at Arcology, time slipped slowly away. Dylan remained in the communications room, racking his brain for a new approach and monitoring the progress of the rest of the team, while Commander Simpson spent some of the time there and some in his own office. Eventually, Simpson came to join Dylan, with a grim expression.

"I've just heard from the Supreme Council of the World Federation," he said. "They seem to have decided that our opponent's bluffing, and they're going to call it. Whatever happens, they won't give in to his demands . . . which leaves it all down to *us* . . ."

"Hmm, well there's not much more we can do as far as the search is concerned," Dylan said, activating his computer console again. "So we'd better go back to the beginning. Let's assume the robbery was carried out by the robot piloting that service-tug yesterday. But that robot's service-recorder shows a perfectly normal routine, so it must have been expertly forged. So we don't even know if it was that robot that carried out the mission. No leads there . . ."

"The service-tug . . ." began Simpson. "It returned to trans-shipping station 4, right. Everything perfectly normal. But how many ships *left* that station in the two or three hours that followed?"

"Three," Dylan told him. "One for Earth, which is one of the ships being investigated now. One for Space Colony 2, and one for the Deep Space Technology Satellite."

"Well, you can forget that last one," said Commander Simpson. "It's run by Paul

Friedrich, an old friend of mine. He'd never get involved in anything like this!''

''Then what about one of his team?'' asked Dylan. ''After all, they use a fair number of robots in their space-construction jobs . . .''

''But there are only three other people up there with Friedrich,'' Simpson told him. ''No, I just can't believe it . . . but I'll give him a call just to make sure . . .''

Paul Friedrich appeared on the visi-screen a few moments later, a big-built man in his late forties with a craggy face and hard staring eyes. But he was friendly and co-operative enough when he saw who was calling, and Dylan sat watching in silence as the man gave a perfectly sound account of his entire team's movements over the last twenty-four hours.

''You see?'' said Simpson when the call was ended. Dylan shrugged.

''I guess it has to be Space Colony 2, then,'' he said, getting to his feet. ''How about me taking up T-bird One and checking it out? There's not a lot else I can do here . . .''

Simpson nodded. ''But if our man sees TB-1 arriving, we're just liable to panic him into setting off his devices. Head for trans-shipping station 4 instead, Dylan . . . I'll commandeer a supply ship for you to make your final approach in . . .''

''Right,'' agreed Dylan, relieved to be getting into the action at last. It was nearly three in the afternoon by the time TB-1 blasted away from Arcology, and there was still no sign of success from the rest of the team.

It was at about that time that Gran put through a call to Jesse and Little John. ''You know, I've been thinking, guys,'' he began. ''We've been using search co-ordinates based on the idea that we're looking for falling space-debris . . . the sort of stuff that comes straight down and smashes into the ground at thousands of miles an hour. But if this is some sort of cannister that's got to be opened later, it'd have to land more gently than that. They'd have to use retro-rockets, parachutes or whatever to slow it down. And if it's coming down more slowly, it'll have a different trajectory . . . and that means a different landing area . . .''

''Too right!'' agreed Jesse. ''Blast! That

means we're going to have to recalculate for an entirely new search-area . . . and so's Kallan. Okay, Gran . . . we're going to get on to Commander Simpson and tap in to the main computers back at Arcology. We'll get back to you as soon as we've got anything . . ."

By the time those new calculations had been made, Dylan had arrived at trans-shipping station 4, and found the supply ship ready and waiting for him. Leaving TB-1 anchored in orbit, he logged a flight-plan for Space-Colony 2 and set off. Then, three miles from the station, he began to change course.

The supply ship moved with frustrating slowness by comparison with Thunderbird One, and it was gone six in the evening by the time Dylan approached the huge, wheel-like Deep Space Technology Satellite. He began to circle it slowly, heading for the vast central docking bay, and at the same time radioing for permission to come alongside.

Landing permission was refused. The reason was plausible enough: a delicate experiment that had to be carried out in a completely vibration-free state, and which couldn't be disturbed by having a supply ship docking . . . but somehow Dylan didn't believe it. It was partly a hunch, partly because the original ultimatum hadn't been delivered by a human voice. Instead, the words had been constructed of a series of electric tonalities, and then cut in on one of the communication satellites. That meant a high level of technology . . . and there wasn't any higher than on this satellite-wheel . . .

But that left Dylan with a big problem. He had to get aboard somehow, and secretly, but without bringing his ship into direct contact with the satellite. He sat back in the pilot chair to think for a moment . . .

"I've found it!" Kallan's voice crackled over the radio excitedly, on the flight-deck of TB-2. "It's a cannister about ten feet long, and showing signs of heat-damage from entry through the atmosphere..."

"Great, Kallan!" replied Jesse, overwhelmed with relief but still trying to keep his mind on the job. "First thing you do is give us the exact co-ordinates. Then by comparing them with the co-ordinates where you were originally searching, we

should get some idea where *we* ought to be looking for *our* cannister. After that . . . don't go near the thing yourself. Use TB-14 on remote control to load it aboard TB-13 . . . and then the lil ol' flying mini-sub can transport it here to Canada to join us . . ."

"Right," agreed Kallan feeding the co-ordinates through directly on the computer. "Keep hunting..."

Up in orbit, high above them, the supply ship turned away from the Technology Satellite and started to head for Space Colony 2, as originally planned. But Dylan was no longer aboard. Dressed in his space-suit, he had set the ship on automatic and sent it on its way, while he used his jet-pack to propel himself through the empty vacuum back toward the wheel. Reaching the outer rim, he found himself a hand-hold and settled down to wait.

Every minute that passed was agonising, but he felt he had to give the supply ship plenty of time to get clear before he tried to make an entrance through one of the airlocks. It was *always* possible to open an emergency airlock, he knew, so there was nothing to stop him getting in. But he wanted to make sure he could do it without anyone else knowing about it.

Half an hour passed before Dylan entered the satellite and stripped off his suit. Then, blaster in hand, he stepped out of the airlock.

But he'd gone no more than a few paces

when he came under fire. Dylan hurled himself around a corner and pressed his back up against the wall as the laser-beams cut the air all around him. There was quite definitely something wrong here, for all Friedrich's assurances to the contrary.

Even more wrong was the fact that he was coming under fire from blaster-toting robots; and robots were supposed to be programmed never to endanger human life. But anyone who could forge a robot's service record was quite capable of over-riding their basic programming too.

But these were ordinary service robots that Dylan was up against, and there was a big difference between re-programming them and making them intelligent. Dylan stuck his blaster round the corner and let off a shot, shoulder-high. Three laser-beams were returned, also shoulder-high.

Then Dylan threw himself out into the corridor, rolling on the floor. Before the robots could readjust their aim, his blaster had fired three times. Three robots went down in a smoking mass of molten metal and smouldering insulation.

Dylan was on his feet instantly and running toward the satellite's control centre. Only one other robot tried to stop him, but he melted it before it had time to aim. Then he was at the satellite's central core, and the door slid open . . .

Friedrich was standing on the other side of the room, with a low control console between them. The scientist turned to face Dylan, thin-lipped and hardeyed, and started to edge slowly toward the console.

''Hold it!'' snapped Dylan, but Friedrich kept walking.

''What will you do?'' he asked, looking Dylan straight in the eye. ''I know you International Rescue people will never kill . . .'' And he took another pace, his hand starting to reach toward the console.

Dylan went down on one knee and shot him straight between the eyes.

As a stench of burning plastic and melting metal filled the air, 'Friedrich' tumbled forward toward the console, a clicking sound in his throat that might almost have been laughter, and pulled a switch before collapsing to the floor. Dylan leaped forward, but it was already too late. All he could do was find a radio and call through a warning to Commander Simpson.

''I took care of our 'man','' he began. ''But just too late . . . he's released the viruses . . .''

''We know, Dylan,'' cut in Jesse suddenly, in less-than-worried tones. ''But we found his cannisters *before* you found him. We're three hundred miles out in space, and we'd just jettisoned the stuff two minutes before it exploded. It's not going to do anyone any harm up here in airless space . . ."

Dylan slumped into a chair, shaking with relief, and sat looking at the smouldering remains of the fake Friedrich for a couple of minutes before going off to find the real man and his companions.

"That's right," explained Friedrich, when Dylan released him from the tiny locked cabin. "We've been working on making an android . . . a perfect robot that not only looks exactly like a human being, but has its own intelligence too. This one was a bit *too* intelligent, though . . . and power-crazed, as well. The first thing it did was lock us up, and then remould its artificial flesh to look like me . . ."

"And it was *that* which carried out the robbery," added Dylan. "It had to be a robot . . . but with a brain of its own . . ."

"Right," agreed Friedrich. "And it would quite happily have wiped out every human being on the planet . . . and then replaced them with androids like itself. There's only one thing that puzzles me . . . how did you know it wasn't me?"

"Observation," said Dylan smiling. "I watched it all the time that Commander Simpson was speaking to it on the visiscreen. The fact that it was always staring gave me the clue . . .

"Artificial eyes don't blink . . ."

THUNDERBIRD CRA

Thunderbird 1

ADVANCED SPACE SHUTTLE

Flight command centre for INTERNATIONAL RESCUE.

NASA design – employs Ultimate Mark 10 HF computer guidance system.

Computer and manned capabilities of this craft allow maximum flexibility for orbital and near-Earth operations.

Length: 62 metres
Weight: 124.8 tons

Thunderbird 3

RECONNAISSANCE GROUND VEHICLE

Mobile multifunctional laboratory and ground operations vehicle.

Can be transported via link-up to TB-1 and TB-2.

The three vehicles together form the nucleus of the THUNDERBIRD rescue force.

Length: 46 metres
Weight: 68.4 tons

T AND EQUIPMENT

Thunderbird 2

HYPERSONIC TRANSPORT

Capable of transporting at ultrahigh speeds any one of many pods containing disaster equipment and/or additional THUNDERBIRD machinery for every conceivable type of emergency.

Giant rocket boosters and twin ion-engine drive give TB-2 the capability for near-Earth and deep space exploration.

TB-1 and TB-3 link onto TB-2 for high-velocity transport to danger zones.

Length: 83 metres
Weight: 193.5 tons

Thunderbird 4

SUBMARINE

TB-4 is capable of descending to depths reachable by no other vehicle and can be airlifted aboard TB-2 for transport anywhere on the Earth or into space should the need arise.

Equipment includes:
Olympic Mark VIII twin electric drive; Twin ultracandescence lighting troughs; Hydraulic ram.

Length: 45 metres
Maximum Cruising Speed: 120 knots (underwater)
96 knots (on surface)
Maximum Diving Depth: 11,000 metres.

Thunderbird 6

SPACE STATION

In L-5 orbit around Earth.

TB-6's Emergency Alert Communications Centre monitors signals from anywhere on Earth or in space. TB-6 houses complete research centre and numerous laboratories and has docking and support facilities for TB-1, TB-2 and TB-3. TB-6 is home to the Construction Coordinators for all UN space colonies. In TB-6's Rescue Operations Control Centre, INTERNATIONAL RESCUE ORGANIZATION scientists and pilots man shifts around the clock, to pin-point emergencies and devise plans for their solution.

Length: 15 km
Weight: 6,200 tons.

Thunderbird 5

SPECIAL GROUND OPERATIONS VEHICLE

Used for fire-fighting and extremely hazardous operations, such as disposal of highly toxic or explosive substances.

Outer shell is constructed of Mandellium, a special alloy that is an extremely efficient insulator and resists temperatures as high as 4,000° Centigrade.

Length: 29 metres
Maximum Speed: 45 km/hr

Thunderbird 7

MINI-AIRCRAFT

High speed. Kept aboard TB-1 for specialized rescue operations and as escape craft.

Specially designed for vertical lift-off and landing.

Length: 12 metres
Weight: 5 tons.

Thunderbird 8

COMPUTER CONTROLLED AIR-TRANSPORT

Stored aboard TB-1, this unmanned aircraft is used for transporting extremely dangerous materials.

Length: 15 metres

Weight: 9 tons

Maximum Speed: Mach 2.

Thunderbird 9

ONE-MAN SPACE WALKERS

TB-9 is used for precision work in outer space.

Full forward thrust; three-axis attitude jets.

Height: 3.5 metres

Weight: 1 ton.

Thunderbird 10

ULTRAHIGH-SPEED MINI-ROCKETSHIP

Used for extremely fast transportation. Can be air-lifted in its pod aboard TB-2.

Length: 18 metres
Weight: 12 tons
Maximum speed: Mach 176.

Thunderbird 11

HIGH-SPEED GROUND VEHICLE

TB-11 is carried aboard TB-3. It is armoured and equipped with computer-controlled sensors and an effective array of weapons.

Length: 5 metres

Weight: 1 ton

Maximum Speed: 370 km/hr (on road surface).

Thunderbird 12

MULTIFUNCTION FLAT BED

TB-12 can be carried aboard TB-3. Equipped with high-powered shovel and extending platform.

Length: 15 metres

Weight: 150 tons

Maximum Speed: 100 km/hr (on road)
40 km/hr (off road)

Thunderbird 13

FLYING MINI-SUB

Carried aboard TB-4.

Length: 9 metres
Maximum Speed in the Atmosphere: Mach 1
Maximum Speed Underwater: 60 knots.

Thunderbird 14

DEEP SEA BATHYSCAPHE

TB-14 can be carried aboard TB-4 when needed for specialized deep-sea operations.

Length: 12 metres
Weight: 5.5 tons
Maximum Speed: 60 knots (submerged).

Thunderbird 15

MOBILE COMPUTER

TB-15 can be remote controlled or manned. Equipped with computer terminals and radio link-up with INTERNATIONAL RESCUE ORGANIZATION central computer. Can be carried aboard TB-5.

Length: 4.5 metres
Weight: 1.9 tons
Maximum Speed: 220 km/hr.

Thunderbird 16

THE MOLE

Remote-controlled digging apparatus. Can be transported aboard TB-5.

Length: 6 metres

Weight: 12 tons

Maximum Speed:

120 km/hr (on surface)
70 km/hr (underwater)

Thunderbird 17

LONG-RANGE SPACE-PROBE

TB-17 is kept aboard Space Terminal, TB-6. Can be radio controlled or can be manned.

Length: 200 metres

Maximum Speed: 27 km/sec

Weight: 1,250 tons.

FOR, FROM THE DEPTHS OF SPACE, **SOMETHING** IS APPROACHING. SOMETHING HUGE AND ALIEN...

AND COLD...

OH SO **VERY** COLD...

FALL OF THE FROST GIANT

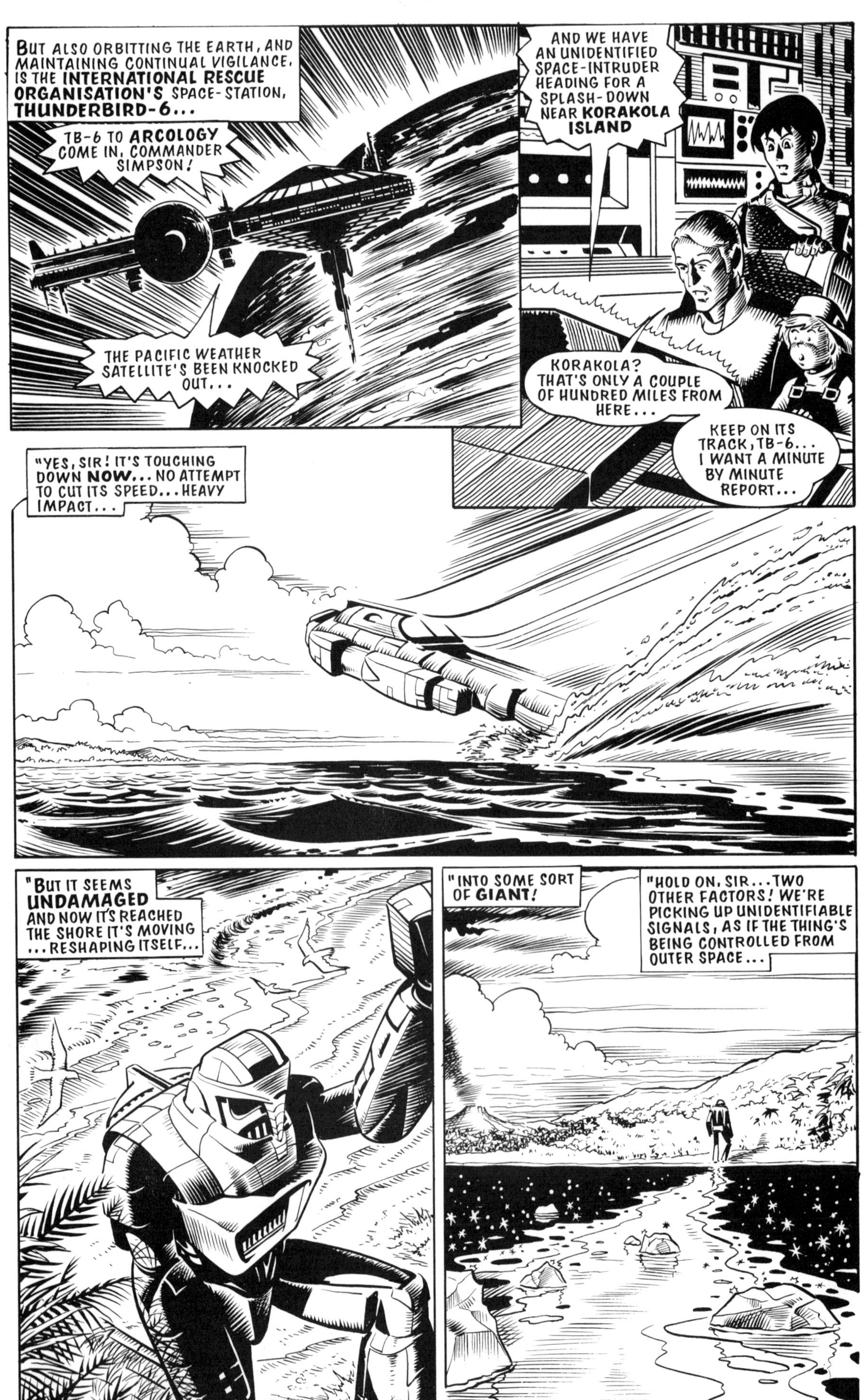
But also orbitting the Earth, and maintaining continual vigilance, is the **International Rescue Organisation's** space-station, **Thunderbird-6...**
TB-6 to **Arcology** come in, Commander Simpson!
The Pacific weather satellite's been knocked out...
And we have an unidentified space-intruder heading for a splash-down near **Korakola Island**
Korakola? That's only a couple of hundred miles from here...
Keep on its track, TB-6... I want a minute by minute report...
"Yes, sir! It's touching down **now**... no attempt to cut its speed... heavy impact...
"But it seems **undamaged** and now it's reached the shore it's moving ...reshaping itself...
"Into some sort of **giant**!
"Hold on, sir... two other factors! We're picking up unidentifiable signals, as if the thing's being controlled from outer space...

"AND WE'RE RECORDING A SUDDEN, ALARMING DROP IN TEMPERATURE!"
FWEESH!
DYLAN... TAKE T-BIRD ONE AND INVESTIGATE! I WANT A CLOSE LOOK AT THAT THING!
ON MY WAY, SIR!
WE'LL FOLLOW UP WITH TB-2 AND TB-3 WHEN WE KNOW WHAT EQUIPMENT WE NEED!
AT LEAST KORAKOLA ISLAND ISN'T INHABITED...
"IS IT?"
MAYDAY! MAYDAY THIS IS ED EDWARDS OF THE BIO-RESEARCH UNIT ON KORAKOLA!
I DON'T KNOW WHAT'S HAPPENING BUT THE TEMPERATURE DROPPED FIFTY DEGREES IN FIVE MINUTES!
SNOW IN THE TROPICS...
ICE IS BUILDING UP! I'M BEING OVERWHELMED...
BURIED...

MEANWHILE...
I CAN SEE IT! NO LIFE-READINGS... AN ALIEN DESIGN...
IT'S MY BET THE THING'S A ROBOT...

PROBABLY SENT FROM AN ULTRA-COLD PLANET TO ALTER OUR CLIMATE...
AND GET EARTH SOFTENED UP FOR AN OFF-WORLD INVASION!

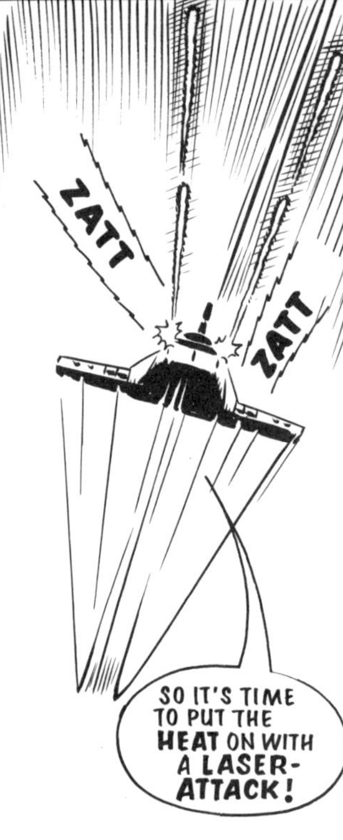
ZATT
ZATT
SO IT'S TIME TO PUT THE HEAT ON WITH A LASER-ATTACK!

BUT...
NO GOOD! IT'S ACTUALLY FREEZING THE AIR TO SHIELD ITSELF...
SHHHK!

AND NOW IT'S SHOOTING BACK!
FWEESH!

GOT TO TAKE EVASIVE ACTION TRY TO LEAD IT AWAY, BECAUSE...

"HERE COME THE OTHER T-BIRDS..."
HEY, YOU SURE THIS IS **KORAKOLA**? NOT THE NORTH POLE?
EDWARDS? ARE YOU STILL OKAY?
Y-YES... I'M... I'M S-STILL H-HERE...
GOOD! KEEP THIS CHANNEL OPEN! WE'LL HOME IN ON YOUR TRANSMITTER!

THUNDERBIRD-16: THE **MOLE**...
HANG ON, ED! WE'RE GOING TO DIG YOU OUT!
D-DIG? B-BUT THAT'LL T-TAKE **HOURS**!

NOT THE WAY **WE** DO IT!
HEY, KALLAN! GET ME A SITUATION REPORT FROM BASE!
SKREEEEE!

THERE'S A TEAM LOOKING AT THE WEATHER SATELLITE ... BUT IT'LL TAKE A **WEEK** TO FIX!
AND BY THAT TIME THE WHOLE PLANET'LL BE **FROZEN SOLID**!

"SO IT'S UP TO YOU **T-BIRDS** TO **DESTROY** THAT THING!
OKAY, LISTEN, EVERYONE! I'VE GOT AN IDEA...

FIRST, I'LL TRY TO LEAD THE THING TO THE FAR END OF THE ISLAND... THEN THAT'S WHERE YOU COME IN...

TB-2
GRAN, KALLAN! YOU HANDLE THIS WE'VE GOT TO GO AND HELP DYLAN!
OKAY, GUYS WE'RE ALMOST THERE!
AND...
SKREEE!
W-WHAT ON EARTH?
OKAY! STOP! STOP OTHERWISE YOU'LL D-DRILL RIGHT THROUGH ME!
THE MOLE'S REMOTE-CONTROLLED, ED... JUST GET ON BOARD AND WE'LL BRING YOU UP!
Y-YOU D-DON'T HAVE TO TELL ME T-TWICE!
WHILE ELSEWHERE...
JESSE... LITTLE JOHN... YOU IN POSITION?
OKAY, LET'S GET STARTED...
SHOULDN'T BE HARD TO PERSUADE OUR FRIGID FRIEND THAT THIS IS A SUICIDE ATTACK... AFTER ALL IT PROBABLY IS...
BUT IF IT GIVES YOU TIME TO GET IN...
ZATT
ZATT

"AND MAKE THE GRAB!"
WE'VE GOT IT!

AND DYLAN PULLED THROUGH OKAY TOO!
SO LET'S HEAD FOR THE VOLCANO FAST!

BUT...
WE'VE LOST A GRAPPLE! THE ROBOT'S SO COLD IT'S MAKING THE METAL BRITTLE!
LET'S HOPE THE OTHER ONE HOLDS OUT UNTIL...

NOW, JESSE! WE'RE OVER THE CRATER! HIT THAT DROP-SWITCH!
DON'T HAVE TO LITTLE JOHN... THE THING'S FALLEN OFF ANYWAY...

BUT RIGHT ON TARGET!
RIGHT INTO THE HEART OF A LIVE VOLCANO!

"LET'S SEE IT TRY TO FREEZE THAT!"
FROOOOOOSH!
AND MOMENTS LATER...
WE'VE DONE IT NOTHING LEFT BUT A HEAP OF SLAG...
AND THE ICE IS ALREADY STARTING TO MELT, TOO! LOOKS LIKE WE'VE GOT IT ALL TIED UP!
AND THE WAY WE TOOK THAT ONE OUT, I CAN'T SEE THEM SENDING ANOTHER!

SOLAR SAILORS

"Now, if I were a betting man," remarked Gran Hansen slowly, "my money would be on Hogan. He's got more grit when the chips are down. If things get tough up there, I'd count on Hogan being the one to pull through . . ."

"Maybe, Gran," put in Little John. "But Gunston's got that much more will to win. He's downright manic about beating Hogan . . ."

"What's going on, everybody?" came a small voice from behind them as Skipper entered the office and found the entire Thunderbirds team gathered round a telescreen. With a flurry of hellos, the group moved aside to let the boy through.

"What kind of spaceships are they, Uncle Warren?" he asked as soon as he could see the screen.

"The kind you only see once every four years, Skipper," Commander Simpson told him. "They're solar space-yachts for the Martian Races . . ."

"They look awfully funny to me," remarked the seven year-old. "Where are the rockets?"

"They don't have any rockets, Skipper," Dylan began to explain, pointing toward the screen and the two fragile, spider-like space-yachts. "See these big sails at the front here? They're covered in solar cells. They pick up the light from the sun and turn it into electricity, which is then run back to the main pod here." And he pointed to a comparatively tiny metal space-capsule, dangling on a frail girder a hundred yards behind the main sails. "That's where the pilot lives and controls the ship . . . and that's where the electricity runs a small ion-drive engine which propels the ship . . ."

"It sounds awful slow," said Skipper dubiously.

"It is to start off with," said Kallan, picking up the explanations. "But as there's no air-resistance out in space, the speed keeps building up all the time the engines are running. They come back from Mars in about half the time it takes them to get there. Even so, it'll be about a year before they return . . ."

"If they get back at all," put in Jesse. "Hardly a race goes by without one of the yachts getting in trouble . . ."

"But there are only two of them!" protested Skipper, unable to come to grips with the idea of men racing in machines so unsafe that there was only a fifty per cent chance of coming through alive.

"Only two this time, Skipper," explained Little John. "It's a special challenge race. Hogan and Gunston. Over the last twenty years they've each won twice . . . the only two men in history to take more than one Martian Pennant. So this one's the clincher. Probably the last chance for either of them to make it three wins. By the time another four years comes round, they'll both be thinking about retiring . . ."

"Maybe they should have retired already," remarked Dylan, suddenly serious. "Sure, it's their own lives they're putting on the line, but if anything goes wrong, we're the ones who have to go out and rescue them. We don't want another disaster like we had twelve years ago . . ."

"Three ships lost without trace," explained Commander Simpson before Skipper got the chance to ask. "That was back before there were any Thunderbirds to pick them up. And that's why we're keeping a close eye on this race. Even if it means tying up time on Thunderbird-6 for a year just keeping them under surveillance . . ."

All of which seemed to explain everything except one last thing. "How come each yacht's got different sails?" asked Skipper.

"They've each got the same area of sail," Gran told him. "But it's up to the pilot what shape he has or how he spreads them . . . whatever he thinks best. That's Hogan who's got the four square sails; Gunston's got the circular one with the hole in the middle. As they'll be heading directly away from the sun at the start of the trip, they always leave a space in the middle where the pod would cast a shadow . . ."

High up in space, in a stationary orbit not far from Thunderbird-6, those sails were fully spread, and after a brief countdown, both Hogan and Gunston turned on their ion-engines at the same time. For many long seconds, absolutely nothing seemed to happen, and then a faint blue glow started to build up behind the engine nacelles, strengthening and brightening gradually as the minutes dragged by. Even so, there was no immediate sign of movement. The acceleration was so slow and gradual that the yachts moved only a few feet in the first ten minutes, and it was half an hour before anyone could see any noticeable difference in their position relative to the International Rescue space-station. The long race was beginning at a speed of less than one mile an hour. As a spectacle it made lousy television, thought Skipper, quickly losing interest in the screen and going off to find something else to do.

Finding something to do was the big problem for Hogan and Gunston too, out on the yachts. For once the course was set, there wasn't a lot of piloting to do. Hogan read space-manuals, Gunston played video-games as the speed rose to a slow walking pace by the end of the day; to that of a run on the second; to that of a cruising car on the third. It was going to be a long, slow way to Mars.

Three weeks passed as the ships drifted slowly further and further out from Earth, Gunston gradually building up a lead of some three or four yards. It wasn't important then, but it might have been later on. By that time too, the swarm of news and TV ships that had been following the yachts had dropped behind, and open space lay before them. A race where nothing happened for weeks on end held little interest to the news media, and Hogan and Gunston would become 'forgotten men' for months . . . until they either approached Mars or until some accident befell one or other of them.

Strangely, two days after the last news-ship was left behind, Gunston's yacht began to drop behind. The loss of speed was minimal: it took six hours for his four yard lead to be wiped out, but over the following days he dropped back still further, until he was running some thirty yards behind Hogan's ship.

Hogan watched all this with a mixture of content and concern. He was obviously pleased with his lead, but on the other hand he had no great desire for Gunston to drop right back and leave him totally alone this early in the race. There was no love lost between the two opponents, especially after the race had been built up as a needlematch, but space is an awfully lonely place. Besides, if something went wrong with a ship so similar to his own, it gave Hogan some cause to worry. The funny thing was, he couldn't see anything amiss with Gunston's yacht . . .

Before long though, something of more immediate concern called for Hogan's attention: his forward scanner began to show a small meteor shower not far ahead. As he started to

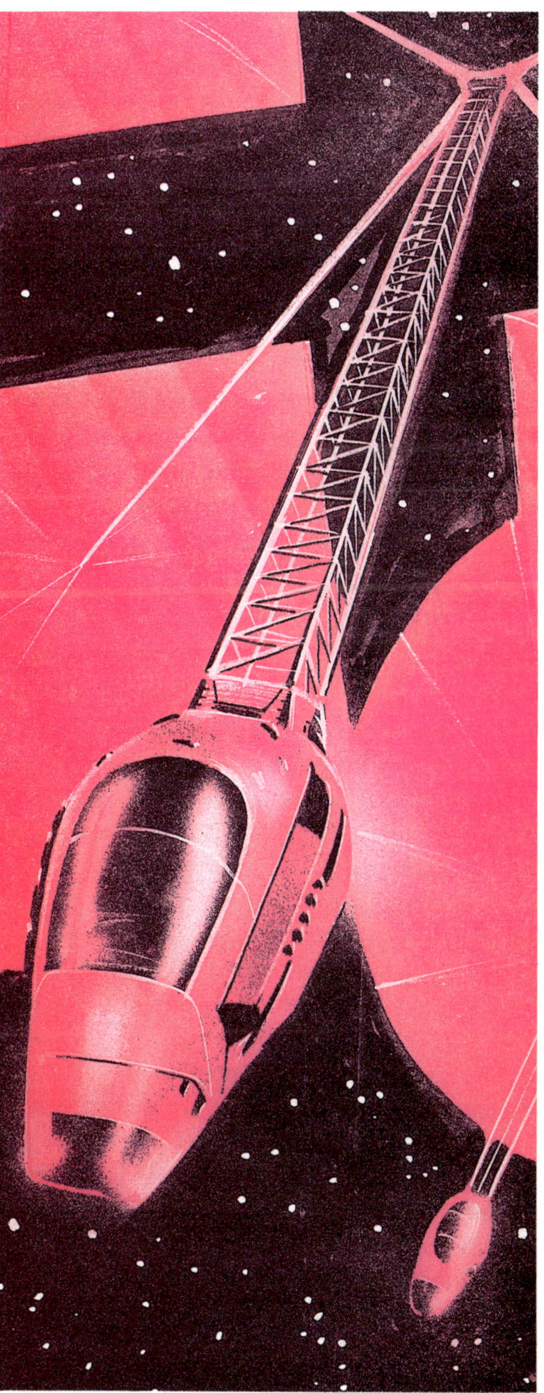

shrug on his space-suit, Hogan put through a radio-call to Gunston, warning him of the danger. After all, there were certain rules to observe, and even if your opponent happened to be your worst enemy, you still didn't leave him to the mercy of a meteor shower. Meteors don't have any.

Funny thing about those meteor showers, reflected Hogan as he snapped his helmet into place and started to breath bottled air. According to the computer-experts, the odds against running into them during this race was sixty to one. And yet three times in the last twenty years, the Martian Racers had run into meteors. They made things interesting, anyway. Even a shower the size of sandparticles could rip a solar sail to pieces, and that would add a human factor to the proceedings. Whoever got out and got his one set of reserve sails rigged fastest would probably win. It was only when the meteors got larger that any real danger came into it, and Hogan had sat tight more than once in the main pod while the things rattled like pebbles against the armoured shell. Something the size of a fist could puncture the pod and put you out of the race. Anything larger than that was liable to put you out of everything, permanently.

According to the scanner, they were running into a fairly small shower. Nothing too dangerous; just a scattering of cosmic debris hanging almost motionless in space. But the yachts would hit them at several hundred miles an hour, and there was no way to manoeuvre round them. Hogan hunched in his seat, waiting for the impact.

The sails went first, naturally. A few small holes appeared to begin with, and then Hogan's right upper sheet suddenly tore to ribbons. The other three sails fell apart almost immediately, and then Hogan heard the pea-sized meteors start to rattle on the walls.

Looking through the armoured port-hole, he could see Gunston's yacht suffering just as badly, its sail disintegrating swiftly as it too ran into the shower. At least they were both in the same trouble.

But not for long. Hogan suddenly froze in horror as he saw his scanner show something large and dangerous drifting toward him. It wasn't moving all that fast, but it was almost as big as the main pod, and something that large didn't have to. Hogan breathed a sigh of relief as his mini-computer indicated a near miss of several yards.

The sigh died on his lips as the scanner showed the giant lump of rock suddenly change course. Hogan knew that ordinary meteors couldn't do that, but he hardly had time to think about it. Within seconds the giant rock was upon him, smashing against the front end of the pod.

The 'meteor' careered straight through the spidery girderwork of the ship, severing the pod from the sails and sending the entire yacht spinning wildly off-course. Hogan felt an explosive rush as the air in the pod escaped, and a large rent appeared in one wall, through which he could see starlight.

Hogan glanced rapidly at the emergency air-bottles. Enough for two or three days if he was lucky, and if the rest of the ship wasn't too badly damaged. The front scanner was out of action though, and he pressed his helmet close to the window. Outside, he saw the giant rock for an instant, and then there was a tiny flash of rocket engines from it. The 'meteor' began to manoeuvre away through empty space.

Hogan reached for the radio. It was dead. That was it, then, he decided. Spinning off course, cut off from any contact; and he was the only one who knew it had been no accident. It was sabotage. It would probably be murder.

In the following yacht, Gunston saw the disaster, and immediately tried to call Hogan on the short-range radio. There was no reply. Worriedly, Gunston switched frequencies and started to put through a distress call to Thunderbird-6.

"I knew it," muttered Dylan, watching the forward screens as Thunderbird-2 climbed out of the Earth's atmosphere and set a course to follow the yachts. "The whole race ought to be banned . . . it's just too dangerous!"

"Maybe," agreed Gran. "But if you tried to stop a sport just because it was risky, where would you end up? Trying to stop people doing everything, just in case something happened . . ."

Dylan shrugged non-commitally and went over to join Kallan as she plotted their course.

"According to Gunston's computer-log, the impact should have taken place here," she remarked, pointing to a graphic chart on the display screen. "Now if we assume that the big meteor had roughly the same motion as the rest of the shower, we can make a rough guess at what vector Hogan's yacht would have moved along after the impact . . . give or take ten degrees. But we don't know the speed, or whether Hogan's engines are still firing, or . . ."

"There are an awful lot of assumptions and guesses and buts in that, Kallan," said Dylan gently. "And even then it leaves us a huge area of space to search. How long till we reach the location of the accident?"

"Four or five hours," said Kallan shrugging. "It's the best we can do right now . . ."

"Okay," Dylan said. "Feed that course through to the main controls. I'm going to check out T-bird One and make sure we're ready to start the search as soon as we arrive . . ."

Gunston was too busy re-rigging his reserve sails to talk to the rescue team for long when they finally arrived, so Thunderbirds One and Two split up and started off at slightly different angles, spreading the search area over a widening cone as they moved away.

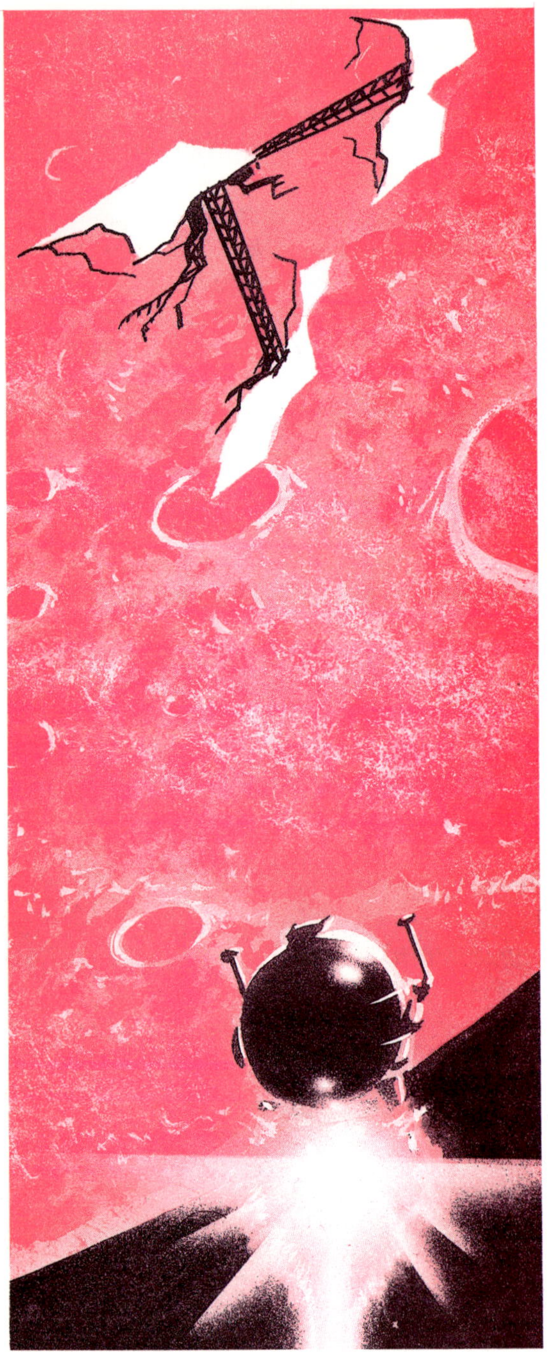

Hogan's yacht was supposed to have an emergency beacon, but they picked up no trace of signals. Either that meant the ship was so badly damaged the beacon had been knocked out, Dylan thought, or that Hogan, in trying to keep his yacht as light as possible, hadn't brought one with him. That broke all the rules in the book, but it wouldn't matter if they couldn't find him. And another hour passed with no sign at all.

In Thunderbird Two Kallan and Gran sat glued to the scanner screens, aching to see something register upon them. But another hour passed with nothing. It was Jesse who made the first sighting, and even then he couldn't believe it.

"Hey, I just saw something dark against the face of the moon!" he exclaimed, staring out of the front window. "Just for a second . . . then it was gone!"

Little John was changing course even before he finished speaking.

"Hey, you're interrupting the search pattern!" protested Kallan, but Little John merely shrugged.

"Maybe," he said. "But I've got a hunch about this. If nothing comes within scanner range in five minutes, we'll pick up the old course . . ."

Four minutes later, though, the scanners did actually show something ahead, but as they moved in closer they found that it was only the severed, tattered sail-assembly from Hogan's ship. Of the main pod there was still no sign, but they dropped a space-beacon and Kallan began recalibrating their search pattern. At least they knew they were on the right track now.

Even so, it took another half an hour to find Hogan, and Thunderbird Two moved in to investigate while Kallan called Dylan to rejoin them.

"The ship's a mess," declared Jesse, looking out the front port. "Ripped open, the airlock shattered. There's no way we can dock with it . . ."

"I'd be surprised if he was still alive in there," said Gran grimly. "But we've got to make sure, Jesse. You and I'll go over in the space-walkers and find out . . ."

Dylan was just bringing Thunderbird One back to dock as the walkers emerged, jets thrusting them toward the crippled yacht. Gran was first to arrive, took a quick look at a rip in the armoured shell, then used the clawended automatic arms of the walker to pull the rip open even wider. Moments later, the arms of Jesse's walker slipped through the gap and, with infinite care, picked up the space-suited Hogan. After only a brief pause while Hogan grabbed his computer-log, Jesse delicately drew the man out through the gap, and they turned to head back to Thunderbird Two.

"I really don't know how to thank you people," said Hogan as he stripped off his space-suit. Dylan looked at him coolly: a man in his late forties, with thick dark hair and a hard craggy face. A man with an obsession.

"Listen, if you've found my sail-rig,"